the Ten Commandments
for children

written by
Ronald L. Cammenga

REFORMED
FREE PUBLISHING
ASSOCIATION

JENISON, MI

Reformed Free Publishing Association
Jenison, Michigan

All Bible quotations are taken from the King James [Authorized] Version

Quotations taken from the Heidelberg Catechism can be found in the *Confessions and the Church Order of the Protestant Reformed Churches*

Lyrics of "Oh, Be Careful" taken from *Let Youth Praise Him!* Copyright © 1944 New Spring Publishing Inc. (ASCAP) (adm.at CapitolCMGPublishing.com) All rights reserved. Used by permission.

Reformed Free Publishing Association
1894 Georgetown Center Drive
Jenison MI 49428
616-457-5970
www.rfpa.org
mail@rfpa.org

Cover and interior design by Erika Kiel

ISBN 978-0-916206-30-7

LCCN 2022949354

To my grandchildren who have learned to obey God's commandments from parents who have taught them, "Blessed are the undefiled in the way, who walk in the law of the LORD" (Psalm 119:1).

Contents

Preface

The Ten Commandments for Children has been written with young children in mind, children ages six to nine. The purpose of the book is to give basic instruction in the Ten Commandments. All the early catechisms of the Protestant Reformation gave instruction in three main areas: the Ten Commandments, the Lord's Prayer, and the Apostles' Creed. This was true of Martin Luther's catechism for children and the catechisms written by John Calvin. Today as never before, there is a need to give our young children basic instruction in these three areas. That is the goal of this book and those that are planned to follow.

Although this book aims to be instructional, it is my hope that it can also be used devotionally. In whatever way you choose to use the book, it is my fervent prayer that you will use it as a means to bring biblically sound teaching of the law of God to your covenant children and grandchildren. May our prayer for them follow the example of the psalmist in Psalm 119:18: "Open thou mine eyes, that I may behold wondrous things out of thy law."

To assist in your instruction, at the end of each chapter I have included discussion questions, a Bible memory verse, and a related psalm to be sung. With the psalm, there is also a psalter number from the 1912 United Presbyterian *Psalter* listed. Below are QR codes which will bring you to the respective apps for the 1912 United Presbyterian *Psalter* on both Android and iOS devices. This psalter can also be found at the website of the Protestant Reformed Churches, www.prca.org.

Android

iOS

1. God's Law

Let's read the
Bible

**Let's read the
Bible**

Exodus 20:1–17

Let's learn a
Bible verse

John 14:15, "If ye love me,
keep my commandments."

Let's listen and learn

"O how love I thy law! It is my meditation all the day." This is what we read in Psalm 119:97. The man who wrote these words—the psalmist—loved God's law. Because he loved God's law, he wanted to obey God's law. He loved God's law so much that he meditated on it throughout the whole day. That means he knew God's law and each of the Ten Commandments that are part of God's law. He thought about what God commands us in his law. He thought about what he should do to obey God's law. And he thought about what he should *not* do because he would be disobeying God's law. He thought about how often he broke God's law because he did not do what God commands in his law. And he thought about how often he broke God's law because he did the things that God's law forbids.

When we sin, we break God's law. This is what sin is. Sin is disobeying God's commandments. Because the law is God's law, when we sin, we disobey God. Sin is always sin against God. Do you know that? Whenever you sin, no matter what your sin is, you are sinning against God. That is what makes our sins so terrible.

God's law is called the Ten Commandments. It is called the Ten Commandments because that is how many commandments there are in God's law. Sometimes God's law is also called the *Decalogue*. Have you ever heard that word? It is a big word, but it is not difficult to understand.

The word Decalogue means "ten words." The Ten Commandments are the ten words or the Decalogue that God gives to us.

God's law—the Decalogue—is found in the Bible in Exodus 20:1–17. In the law, God commands us to do certain things and not to do other things. In the Ten Commandments, God calls us to be a certain kind of people and to live a certain way. If we love God, we will want to obey him. And if we want to obey him, we will try to obey his law.

That's the way it is in your earthly life, isn't it? If you love your parents, you obey them. If you love your teacher at school, you obey her. If you love your country, you obey its laws. It is that way with God and God's law, too. Keeping God's commandments is the proof that you love him. And if you love him, you will keep his commandments.

Let's talk it over

1. What is God's law?

2. What does the word Decalogue mean?

3. Fill in the blank:
   "If you love God, you will
   _____."

Let's sing

Psalm 1, Psalter 1 in the 1912 United Presbyterian *Psalter*

2. The Ten Commandments

Let's read the Bible

Psalm 119:1–8

Let's learn a Bible verse

Psalm 119:47, "And I will delight myself in thy commandments, which I have loved."

Let's listen and learn

There are ten commandments in God's law. There are not nine commandments; there are not twelve commandments. There are ten commandments. There is a very important reason that the number of commandments in God's law is ten. The number ten is important in the Bible.

Ten is the number of completeness. God sent ten plagues on the nation of Egypt. Through the ten plagues, God completely destroyed the Egyptians. Jesus told a parable about ten virgins. God gave you ten fingers and ten toes. That is just the right number. It would not be good if you were missing some of your fingers or toes. And it would not help you to have extra fingers or toes. That's the way it is with God's law. Ten is the perfect number of commandments.

The Ten Commandments can be divided almost in half. God showed that when he gave the law to the children of Israel. God wrote some of the commandments on one stone tablet, and he wrote the rest on a second stone tablet.

On the first tablet, or table, of the law, God wrote commandments one through four. These commandments tell us how we are to live with God. They are about our calling toward God. These commandments are first because God must always be first in our lives. The most important thing in your life must be God and obedience to him. Nothing may come before obedience to God.

On the second tablet, God wrote commandments five through ten. These commandments tell us how we are to live with our neighbor. Our neighbor is anyone whom God puts into our lives. Our neighbors begin with the other members of our family. But our neighbors are also the other children at school and the people who live in the house next door. In the end, our neighbors are all the other people who live around us and whom we come to know. On the second tablet, or table of the law, we are taught how we are to live with these neighbors.

Taken together, the Ten Commandments tell us every important truth about how we are to live with God our Creator and Savior, and how we are to live with those whom God has put into our lives. In the next chapters, we want to look more closely at how we are to live with God and how we are to live with our neighbor.

Let's talk it over

1. Into how many parts is God's law divided?

2. What is the difference between the two parts of God's law?

3. Who are some of your neighbors?

Let's sing

Psalm 119, Psalter 333 in the 1912 United Presbyterian *Psalter*

3. Why Has God Given Us His Law?

Let's read the Bible

Colossians 3:17–25

Let's listen and learn

In order to understand why God has given his law to us, it is important to remember when God gave his law to the children of Israel.

God did not give his law to the children of Israel while they were slaves in Egypt. God gave them his law after he had delivered them out of Egypt. God was showing the children of Israel something. He did not deliver them out of Egypt because they had earned their deliverance by obeying his law. Rather, he delivered them out of Egypt so that

they might keep his law. They were called to keep God's commandments because he had delivered them.

God reminded the children of Israel of this in the first part of the law: "I am the Lord thy God, which have brought thee out of the land of Egypt, out of the house of bondage" (Exodus 20:2). Before God gave the law, he called his people to remember his mighty deliverance of them.

This teaches us the reason God gives the Ten Commandments to us today. We often say that we are called to keep God's law out of *gratitude*, or thankfulness. When someone gives you a gift, you tell them thank you. God has given us the greatest gift—salvation. The children of Israel's deliverance out of Egypt was a picture of God's salvation of us from sin and death, Satan and hell.

God gives us the Ten Commandments so that we can show him our thankfulness for this deliverance. We were slaves, too. But by saving us, God delivers us out of our spiritual slavery, just as he delivered the children of Israel out of the slavery of Egypt. We have our deliverance in Jesus. He died on the cross to set us free. Now that we have been set free, we are called to show thankfulness to God by keeping his commandments.

Children, you can understand this. Why do you obey your parents? Why do you do what pleases them? Why do you pick up your toys, clean your room, set the table, sweep the floor, help with the dishes, and bring out the trash? Do you do all these things because you want your dad and mom to become your parents? Or do you obey them because they are your parents, and because you want to show how glad you are that God gave them to be your parents? We all know the answer to these questions. That is also why we keep God's law. By obeying him, we show how glad we are that he is our Father and we are his children.

Let's learn a Bible verse

Colossians 3:17, "And whatsoever ye do in word or deed, do all in the name of the Lord Jesus, giving thanks to God and the Father by him."

Let's talk it over

1. When did God give the Ten Commandments to the children of Israel?

2. What is gratitude? What is another word for gratitude?

3. Do we keep God's commandments to earn something from God, or to show our gratitude to God?

Let's sing

Psalm 30, Psalter 77 in the 1912 United Presbyterian *Psalter*

4. Knowing Our Sins

Let's read the Bible

Revelation 21:1–8

Let's learn a Bible verse

Romans 3:20b, "For by the law is the knowledge of sin."

Let's sing

Psalm 51, Psalter 140 in the 1912 United Presbyterian *Psalter*

Let's listen and learn

The most important reason for keeping God's commandments is to show our gratitude to him for our salvation. But this is not the only reason God wills that we strive to obey his law. There are some other important reasons. We will look at these reasons in this chapter and in the next two chapters.

One important reason we must strive to obey God's law is to learn how sinful we are. This is one of God's purposes when ministers preach and teach his law in church.

Whenever we try to obey God's commandments, we never obey them perfectly. We never do! We never worship God perfectly. We never obey our parents perfectly. We never treat others the way we should, whether they are our classmates or the other members of our family. As long as we are in this life, we will never obey God's law perfectly. We will always fall short of perfect obedience.

Understanding our sinfulness has two results. The first result is that we continually go to our Savior, the Lord Jesus Christ, for the forgiveness of our sins. God's law makes our weaknesses and sins very clear. And that drives us to the cross of Jesus Christ because it is in him alone that we have the forgiveness of our sins. He is the only one who has ever kept God's law perfectly. He is the only one who loved God above all else and his neighbor as himself. And he is the one who suffered all the wrath of God to pay for our

disobedience to God's law. That is what he did on the cross. That is what his cross was. It was Jesus Christ enduring God's judgment in our place, for all of our disobedience. The teaching of the law makes us see what great sinners we are.

The preaching and teaching of God's law also causes us to look forward to going to heaven. This is the second result of understanding our sinfulness. Only in heaven will we keep God's law perfectly. Only in heaven will we love God and enjoy his fellowship perfectly. And only in heaven will we love our neighbor and seek his good perfectly. At last we will serve God without any more sin! How wonderful heaven will be!

Let's talk it over

1. Besides showing our thankfulness to God, what is another important reason for striving to obey God's law?

2. Who was the only one ever to obey God's law perfectly?

3. What is one of the most important reasons that the child of God wants to go to heaven?

5. Letting Our Light Shine

Let's read the Bible

1 Peter 2:1–12

In the last couple of chapters, we have been talking about why we obey God's law. The first and most important reason is to show our thanks to God for our salvation. The second reason is that we want to learn how sinful we are so that we look to Jesus Christ alone for all our salvation. In this chapter, we want to learn another reason for obeying God's law. The reason is that we may let our light shine in the dark and sinful world.

16

That is what Jesus says in Matthew 5:16: "Let your light so shine before men, that they may see your good works, and glorify your Father which is in heaven." Good works are those things that we do in obedience to God's law and to glorify his name. When we obey God's law, we do good works and let our light shine in the world. And when we let our light shine, we are witnessing to others of God. A *witness* is someone who tells others about God.

The light that shines when we obey God's law is seen by the people who live around us; it is especially by the ungodly. Sometimes God uses our good works to turn ungodly people away from their sins and toward him. When the ungodly turn from their sin, they glorify our Father who is in heaven. When this happens, it is a very wonderful thing. The apostle Peter wrote that sometimes the wicked "may by your good works, which they behold, glorify God" (1 Peter 2:12).

This doesn't always happen, though. Sometimes when the ungodly see that we obey God's law, they mock us. Sometimes they become angry and persecute us. They may put us in prison. They may even put us to death. There have been people of God who have died because they obeyed God's law. That happened to Abel, one of the sons of Adam and Eve. Because he obeyed and served God, his wicked brother Cain killed him. The Bible says that Cain killed his brother Abel "because his own works were evil, and his brother's [were] righteous" (1 John 3:12). This also happened to Stephen, one of the first deacons in the New Testament church, when he preached that Jesus was the Messiah (Acts 7:59–60).

Even though others see us when we let our light shine, the most important reason for letting our light shine is that God sees us. When God sees our light shining in the dark and sinful world, he is glorified.

Let's learn a Bible verse

Psalm 119:127, "Therefore I love thy commandments above gold; yea, above fine gold."

Let's talk it over

1. How do Christians let their light shine in the world?

2. Have you ever been poked fun of or teased because you would not do something wrong or because you did what was right?

3. Have you ever stood up for someone who was poked fun of or teased because they would not do something wrong or because they did what was right?

Let's sing

Psalm 67, Psalter 176 in the 1912 United Presbyterian *Psalter*

6. Knowing That We Are God's Children

Let's read the Bible

1 John 2:1–8

Let's learn a Bible verse

1 John 2:3, "And hereby we do know that we know him, if we keep his commandments."

Let's sing

Psalm 15, Psalter 25 in the 1912 United Presbyterian *Psalter*

Let's listen and learn

"Why should we obey God's law?" That is the question we have been answering in the last few chapters. The most important reason is to show our thankfulness to God because he has saved us from our sins. We also have seen that when we try to obey God's commandments, we learn more and more how sinful we are. When the law shows us our sinfulness, we learn to put our trust in Jesus for salvation, and not in ourselves. He is the only one who has ever obeyed God's law perfectly. Another important reason for obeying God's law is to let our light shine in this wicked world. When we obey God's law, we show to others that we are God's children.

There is one more important reason that we obey God's commandments. When we obey the law, God assures us that we are the children of God. *Assurance* means to be sure of something. The word "sure" is part of the word assurance. When you have the assurance of something, you know that it is true. You have no doubt about it. Children should have the assurance that their parents love them. They should have no doubt about that. God uses our good works to assure us that he is our God and we are his people. This assurance is also called knowing God. How can we know that we know God? The apostle John put it like this: "And hereby we do know that we know him, if we keep his commandments" (1 John 2:3). When we keep

God's commandments and do good works, God strengthens our assurance.

Does this mean that we know God and we are saved *because* we obey his commandments? No. Every child of God knows that he obeys God's law only because God works that obedience in him. We would never obey God's law if we were left to ourselves. The prophet Isaiah said in Isaiah 26:12, "For thou [LORD] also hast wrought all our works in us." When we feel the desire in our hearts to obey God's law, we know that this desire is from God. The apostle Paul wrote in Philippians 2:13, "For it is God which worketh in you both to will and to do of his good pleasure." Both our willing and our doing of good works is due to God's work in us. When we desire to obey God's law and when we do obey God's law, we can know that God is working in us. And that ought to make us even more thankful to him for the blessings he bestows on us.

Let's talk it over

1. What does it mean that we know that we know God? (See 1 John 2:3.)

2. How may the child of God be assured of his salvation?

3. What does this mean for us if we live in disobedience to God's law?

19

7. The Law of Love

Mark 12:30–31, "And thou shalt love the Lord thy God with all thy heart, and with all thy soul, and with all thy mind, and with all thy strength: this is the first commandment. And the second is like, namely this, thou shalt love thy neighbour as thyself. There is none other commandment greater than these."

Let's sing

Psalm 116, Psalter 312 in the 1912 United Presbyterian *Psalter*

Once during Jesus' earthly ministry, a man asked, "Master, which is the great commandment in the law?" (Matthew 22:36). The verse just before says that the man asked this question of Jesus, "tempting him." The man wasn't really interested in an answer to his question. He wanted to trap Jesus in his words so that he could convince the people that Jesus was not the Messiah, the Son of God. The man thought he could trick Jesus into giving a wrong answer. Instead, Jesus gave a beautiful answer. He said, "Thou shalt love the Lord thy God with all thy heart, and with all thy soul, and with all thy mind. This is the first and great commandment. And the second is like unto it, thou shalt love thy neighbor as thyself. On these two commandments hang all the law and the prophets" (Matthew 22:37–40).

Jesus did not pick one of the Ten Commandments and make that commandment more important than all the rest. That is what the man wanted Jesus to do so that he could accuse Jesus of being a false teacher. Instead, Jesus pointed to the commandment that stands behind all the other commandments: love God with all your heart, soul, mind, and strength. We usually refer to Jesus' words as the "summary of the law" or the "principle of the law."

The Ten Commandments call us to love God. This, says Jesus, is the first and great commandment. The Ten Commandments also call us to love our neighbor. In Romans 13:10, the apostle Paul says that our love for our

neighbor means that we will not do any wrong to him. This is why Paul also wrote that "love is the fulfilling of the law." The "neighbor" whom you are to love is anyone whom God puts into your life. The members of your family are your first neighbors—your parents and brothers and sisters. Your classmates at school, the people who belong to your church, the people who live next door to you, the people with whom you will someday work or go to college—these are all your neighbors. God's law calls you to love God and love your neighbor.

Love and law go together. If we love God, we will keep his commandments. If a man despises God's law, it is because he does not love God—in fact, he hates God. The apostle John says that "this is the love of God, that we keep his commandments" (1 John 5:3). And Jesus exhorts his disciples in John 14:15, "If ye love me, keep my commandments." Whoever truly loves God, wants to keep God's commandments.

Let's talk it over

1. What is the first and great commandment of God's law?

2. Who is your neighbor? What is your calling toward your neighbor?

3. Do you know what a hypocrite is? What is the difference between a hypocrite and a true child of God?

8. The First Commandment: Flee Idolatry!

Let's read the Bible

Psalm 115:1–11

Let's listen and learn

The first commandment of God's law is, "Thou shalt have no other gods before me" (Exodus 20:3). The first commandment calls us to worship God alone. We are to worship God alone because he *is* God alone. There are no other gods besides God. He is the true God and the only God. We are to show our love for God by worshiping him and trusting in him alone.

The first commandment condemns the sin of idolatry. Idolatry is worshiping another god instead of God or worshiping the true God and another god. It is also idolatry

to trust in any other god than the Lord God. This was the sin that God's people fell into often in the Old Testament. Soon after God delivered the children of Israel from Egypt, at the very time that God was giving Moses the Ten Commandments on Mt. Sinai, the people began worshiping a golden calf. Wicked King Jeroboam built golden calves, too: one in Bethel and one in Dan. And another wicked king, Ahab, and his evil wife Jezebel, introduced the worship of Baal into Israel. The Israelites would also follow the wicked nations around them and worship the sun, moon, and stars. Some of Israel's kings even taught the people to worship Molech, an idol to whom little babies were sacrificed! How awful is that!

In the New Testament, there are many warnings against the sin of worshiping other gods than the Lord God. Romans 1 talks about God's judgment on those who "changed the glory of the uncorruptible God into an image made like to corruptible man, and to birds, and four-footed beasts, and creeping things" (Romans 1:23). This is why Paul warned in 1 Corinthians 10:14, "Wherefore, my dearly beloved, flee from idolatry" and why the apostle John ended his first epistle with the warning, "Little children, keep yourselves from idols" (1 John 5:21).

Just because we don't bow down to idols made of wood or stone, we must not suppose that we do not commit the sin of idolatry. All you need to do is to ask yourself, "Do I trust in God? Do I trust in God alone? Do I trust in God to care for me and my family? Do I trust that he will make whatever happens to me turn out for my good?" We show our love for God by worshiping, fearing, trusting in, and obeying him alone.

Let's learn a Bible verse

Luke 4:8b, "Thou shalt worship the Lord thy God, and him only shalt thou serve."

Let's talk it over

1. What is the sin of idolatry?

2. Can you think of any idols that are mentioned in the Bible?

3. In what ways can we be guilty of breaking the first commandment?

Let's sing

Psalm 115, Psalter 308 in the 1912 United Presbyterian *Psalter*

9. The First Commandment: Worship God Alone!

Let's read the Bible

Psalm 100

Psalm 100:3, "Know ye that the LORD he is God: it is he that hath made us, and not we ourselves; we are his people, and the sheep of his pasture."

The first commandment forbids the sin of idolatry. We may not have another god instead of or in addition to the true God. But the first commandment does not only condemn the sin of idolatry. It also calls us to worship faithfully the one true God alone!

Who is the one true God whom we worship? That is one of the most important questions that you can ask. What is your answer?

In giving your answer, it is important that you start with the Bible. In the Bible, God makes himself known to us. People who reject the Bible cannot truly know God, so they cannot obey the first commandment. Only those who read the Bible can truly know God and keep his commandments. That is why it is so important that we read and study the Bible every day. From the Bible, we learn who God is. From the Bible, we learn all about him and his great works. God is both our Creator and our Father for Jesus' sake. These are the two most important things that we must know about God.

Both of these truths are mentioned in Psalm 100:3: "Know ye that the LORD he is God: it is he that hath made us, and not we ourselves; we are his people, and the sheep of his pasture." "The LORD," says the psalmist, "he is God." He is our God because "he hath made us." And he is our God because he has made us "his people, and the sheep of his pasture."

This is the God whom we are to love, worship, and obey, as the first commandment teaches. This is the God to whom we are to pray and whose word we are to hear. When you gather with your family for devotions, or when your teacher at school has devotions with your class, this is the God you are serving. When you get on your knees by the side of your bed before going to sleep at night, this is the God to whom you are praying. When you go to church with your parents and brothers and sisters and the rest of God's people who belong to your congregation, this is the God you are adoring and praising. When your minister preaches on Sunday, this is the God about whom he is preaching and whose word he is proclaiming. You are listening to God speak to you. Remind yourself of this when you are in church on Sunday.

Let's talk it over

1. Who is God?

2. Where do we learn about God?

3. What are the different ways in which we worship God?

Let's sing

Psalm 100, Psalter 268 in the 1912 United Presbyterian *Psalter*

10. The Second Commandment: No Graven Images!

Let's read the Bible

Isaiah 44:9–20

Let's listen and learn

The second commandment is, "Thou shalt not make unto thee any graven image, or any likeness of anything that is in heaven above, or that is in the earth beneath, or that is in the water under the earth: thou shalt not bow down thyself to them, nor serve them: for I the LORD thy God am a jealous God, visiting the iniquity of the fathers upon the children unto the third and fourth generation of them that hate me; and shewing mercy unto thousands of them that love me, and keep my commandments" (Exodus 20:4–6).

We obey God's law out of love and thankfulness. There is a group of words that we find several times in the Ten Commandments that makes this plain. We find these words first in the second commandment. The group of words is "the Lord *thy* God." These words are also found in the third, the fourth, and the fifth commandments, and they are found in the summary of the law. The Lord is not just *the* God. He is *our* God. In the Old Testament, he was Israel's God in a way in which he was not the God to any other people: not to the Egyptians, not to the Philistines, and not to any of the nations in the land of Canaan. And he is our God today in a way in which he is not the God of the wicked world. Because God is our God, we ought to love and serve him.

But how are we to show God our thankfulness and love? How are we to worship him? The second commandment answers that question. We are *not* to worship God by making and bowing down to an image of wood or stone. That is absolutely forbidden. This is how the heathen always worship their gods. They always make an image that they can see, to which they pray, and before which they bow down in worship. The psalmist in Psalm 135 wrote about the folly of worshiping an image: "The idols of the heathen are silver and gold, the work of men's hands. They have mouths, but they speak not; eyes have they, but they see not; they have ears, but they hear not; neither is there any breath in their mouths" (vv. 15–17).

Very often in their history, the Israelites worshiped God by making an image. They wrongly supposed that this would help them in their worship of God. And throughout history, there have always been those who have made images of God or of Jesus to help them in their worship. But the second commandment forbids the worship of God by images. It is not enough that we worship God; we must worship him *in the right way*. That way is not by an image.

Let's learn a Bible verse

John 4:24, "God is a Spirit: and they that worship him must worship him in spirit and in truth."

Let's talk it over

1. In your own words, what is the second commandment of God's law?

2. What is the meaning of these words in the second commandment: "the Lord *thy* God"?

3. Can you think of examples from the Bible of times when people wrongly worshiped God by images?

Let's sing

Psalm 97, Psalter 260 in the 1912 United Presbyterian *Psalter*

11. The Second Commandment: Worship God through His Word!

Let's read the Bible

Romans 10:13–21

Let's learn a Bible verse

1 Corinthians 1:18, "For the preaching of the cross is to them that perish foolishness; but unto us which are saved it is the power of God."

Let's sing

Psalm 119, Psalter 322 in the 1912 United Presbyterian *Psalter*

Let's listen and learn

The first commandment teaches us whom we are to worship: we are to worship the one true God. The second commandment builds on the first commandment and teaches us how we are to worship the one true God. We are *not* to worship him by making and bowing down to an image. Instead, we are to worship him through his word. That is the meaning of the second commandment. The Heidelberg Catechism explains the second commandment by saying that "we must not pretend to be wiser than God, who will have his people taught, not by dumb images, but by the lively preaching of his word" (Lord's Day 35). God has revealed himself in his word. It is not from an image, but out of the Bible that he wants us to learn about him.

That means that we must read and study God's word faithfully. Before you are able to read the word of God on your own, your parents and grandparents, your older brothers and sisters, your minister, and your teachers must read and explain the word of God to you. Perhaps this is how you learned to read or how you are learning to read, by reading a verse or two out of the Bible at the time when your family had devotions together. In 2 Timothy 3:15, we read that "from a child," Timothy knew the holy Scriptures.

But the second commandment does not only include the reading of the word of God. It also includes the preaching of God's word by the minister in church on Sunday. That is very important! The apostle Paul says in Titus 1:3 that

God has "manifested his word through preaching." We must hear the preaching of God's word every week, usually twice every Sunday, if we are going to keep the second commandment. Apart from the preaching of God's word, we cannot properly know God and worship him. That's why God sent his prophets to his people in the Old Testament. That's why Jesus preached to the people who lived during his ministry. That's how the apostles did their work. That is still true today. God gathers and builds up his church by the preaching of the gospel. The gospel speaks of what God has done, is doing, and promises yet to do through Jesus Christ our Savior. All our lifetime, from the time we are little children until we are very old, God uses the preaching of the gospel to plant and to nourish faith in our hearts.

This makes going to church and listening to the minister very important. When we are in church and listening to the minister preach, we are listening to the voice of our Lord Jesus Christ. Will you remember that when you go to church next Sunday?

Let's talk it over

1. Can you explain the difference between the first and second commandments?

2. How are we to worship God?

3. Do you listen carefully to the preaching of God's word on Sunday? What could you do to improve how well you listen to sermons?

29

12. The Third Commandment: Don't Abuse God's Holy Name!

Let's read the Bible

Psalm 29

Let's learn a Bible verse

Psalm 29:2, "Give unto the Lord the glory due unto his name; worship the Lord in the beauty of holiness."

Let's sing

Psalm 113, Psalter 306 in the 1912 United Presbyterian *Psalter*

Let's listen and learn

The third commandment is, "Thou shalt not take the name of the Lord thy God in vain; for the Lord will not hold him guiltless that taketh his name in vain" (Exodus 20:7). This is a very brief commandment—only one sentence. But it is a very important commandment because it has to do with God's name. The commandment teaches us, "Don't abuse the holy name of God with your tongues and words!" Instead we must use our tongues and words to glorify God's name.

What is the name of God? God has many names. They tell us about himself, his greatness, and his glory. God tells us these things in the Bible. The name *God* means almighty. God is not only mighty; he is almighty. He rules over all things, including his enemies. The name *Jehovah* means "I am." God is unchangeable. He never says "I was" or "I shall be," but always "I am." His love for us never changes, even when we sin against him. He is also Lord. As Lord, he rules over all things so that what he wills always comes to pass.

We have been given our names. Parents give names to their children because they have authority over them. But no one gives God his names. That makes God different from all the idols in this world. Idols are given names by those who worship them. That's not true of God.

There are many ways in which it is possible to break the third commandment and abuse God's holy name. All blasphemy and cursing are forbidden by the third

commandment. When someone hits their finger with a hammer and then damns the hammer, that is cursing. To damn is to send someone to hell. Only God has the right to send people to hell. We also break the third commandment by carelessly using God's attributes like holiness and grace in our speech. People might say, "Holy cow!" or "Goodness gracious!" when they are surprised. These are both abuses of God's name. Only God is holy, and only God is gracious.

There are times when we do not actually abuse God's holy name, but we still sin against the third commandment. How? When someone abuses God's name, and we say nothing, we break the third commandment. For this reason, we must choose our friends carefully. We must not be friends with those who take God's holy name in vain. We also must be careful when we watch television, play video games, and use the internet. Never may we be entertained by those who drag God's holy name through the mud. We love God too much to allow this to happen.

Let's talk it over

1. In your own words, what is the third commandment of God's law?

2. What is the name of God? What is so special about the name of God?

3. What are some ways in which the name of God is abused? What are some ways in which you break the third commandment?

13. The Third Commandment: Be Careful Little Tongue What You Say!

Let's read the Bible

Leviticus 24:10–16

"Oh, be careful, little tongue, what you say, oh, be careful, little tongue, what you say, for the Father up above is looking down in love, so be careful, little tongue, what you say." That is a stanza from a song for young children. This song warns against breaking the third commandment. It also tells us that we must be careful when we use our tongues to worship God.

The third commandment tells us *how* we are to worship God. We are to worship God by using his name reverently. When we speak to each other at home and school, when we play, and as we go about our life in the world, we must always use God's name reverently.

One important way in which we use the name of God is in prayer. We pray before we start our day and when we go to bed at night. We pray before and after our meals. We pray with our parents, with our Christian school teachers, and on our own. Often we are not speaking the words of the prayer aloud, but someone else is, like our father or mother, our minister, or our teacher. Then we must listen and make their prayer our own. If we do not, we take God's name in vain.

One very important place where we must properly use the name of God is in church. The third commandment forbids the vain—or thoughtless—use of God's name. Where does this take place? When is God's name used thoughtlessly? The answer: often in church on Sunday. This is really the most serious sin against the third commandment.

How are we tempted to sin against the third commandment in church? We can use God's holy name without thinking. When we sing his praises, we do not think about the words of the song. During the congregational prayer, we do not pay attention to the words of the minister as he leads us in prayer. Maybe we are even sleeping. When God's word is read, we think about other things. When the minister preaches the gospel of Jesus Christ, we are not listening.

We must pray to God to forgive our thoughtless use of his name. And we must pray to God for the grace to use his name reverently. How can we use God's name reverently? We can only use the name of God reverently when we remember that Jesus is the great name of God. His name means "Jehovah salvation." The third commandment calls us to believe on Jesus, to put our trust in Jesus, and to worship and serve him.

Let's learn a Bible verse

Psalm 115:1, "Not unto us, O LORD, not unto us, but unto thy name give glory, for thy mercy, and for thy truth's sake."

Let's talk it over

1. What is the very worst sin against the third commandment? Are you guilty of this sin?

2. In what different ways can we use God's holy name properly?

3. What does the third commandment have to do with the worship of God in church?

Let's sing

Psalm 28, Psalter 75 in the 1912 United Presbyterian *Psalter*

14. The Fourth Commandment: Remember the Sabbath Day!

Let's read the Bible

Psalm 122

Let's learn a Bible verse

Psalm 27:8, "When thou saidst, Seek ye my face; my heart said unto thee, Thy face, LORD, will I seek."

Let's sing

Psalm 22, Psalter 51 in the 1912 United Presbyterian *Psalter*

Let's listen and learn

The fourth commandment is, "Remember the sabbath day, to keep it holy. Six days shalt thou labor, and do all thy work: but the seventh day is the Sabbath of the LORD thy God: in it thou shalt not do any work, thou, nor thy son, nor thy daughter, thy manservant, nor thy maidservant, nor thy cattle, nor thy stranger that is within thy gates: for in six days the LORD made heaven and earth, the sea, and all that in them is, and rested the seventh day: wherefore the LORD blessed the sabbath day, and hallowed it" (Exodus 20:8–11).

The sabbath day, which is the same as Sunday, is a very special day. In the fourth commandment, God has set this day apart from all the other days of the week. We are to "remember" the sabbath day, and we are to "keep it holy."

We are to keep the sabbath day holy by worshiping God on this day. In Genesis 1, God set this day apart after the six days in which he had created everything. This is one thing that we are to remember on Sunday. But there is another wonderful thing that we remember on this day. Sunday was the day on which our Lord Jesus Christ rose from the dead.

One of the main ways in which we remember the sabbath day and keep it holy is by not doing our ordinary work. The commandment says, "Six days shalt thou labor, and do all thy work," but on the Lord's day "thou shalt not do any work."

The point of the fourth commandment is that we are not to do our ordinary work, the work we do the other six days

34

of the week. When we are young, that work may be our schoolwork, cleaning our room, or mowing the lawn. When we become older, that work is our job or career. Whatever ordinary work God gives us in this world, we set it aside on the sabbath day in order to worship God.

More is included in the fourth commandment than laying aside our ordinary work. The Bible teaches that we are also not to spend Sunday doing our ordinary play or recreation. God's prophet Isaiah rebuked the Israelites in the Old Testament for doing their own pleasure on the Sabbath. He called them to honor God on the Sabbath by "not doing thine own ways, nor finding thine own pleasure, nor speaking thine own words" (Isaiah 58:13). We can also desecrate the Sabbath by playing basketball or golf, going hunting or fishing.

We may not spend Sunday like any other day of the week because Sunday is not like any other day of the week. Sunday belongs to God in a special way. Even though all the days of the week belong to him, God has given six days of the week to us for work and for play. But Sunday is different. Sunday is the Lord's day. Sunday is a day set apart for the worship of God.

Let's talk it over

1. In your own words, what is the fourth commandment of God's law?

2. What is the great purpose of the fourth commandment?

3. What two things are forbidden by the fourth commandment?

15. The Fourth Commandment: Worship the Lord!

Let's read the Bible

Matthew 12:1–13

Let's learn a Bible verse

Psalm 122:1, "I was glad when they said unto me, Let us go into the house of the LORD."

Let's sing

Psalm 36, Psalter 94 in the 1912 United Presbyterian *Psalter*

Let's listen and learn

"Remember the sabbath day, to keep it holy" (Exodus 20:8). The fourth commandment has to do with the special day that God has set aside for the public worship of his name. It is the day on which we go to church in order to sing God's praises, to pray, to fellowship with his people, to give our offerings, and above all, to hear his word.

God intends Sunday to be a day of rest. *Sabbath* means rest. God made us in such a way that we need a certain amount of rest. We usually get that rest in bed at night. We wake up in the morning refreshed—able to take up our work in a new day. But the sabbath day is a special day of rest. It has been made by God as a day of rest, not only for our bodies, but also for our souls. It has been made by God as a day of spiritual rest. God knows that we need that kind of rest, too. We need rest from our constant struggle against sin. We need rest from all the heavy burdens that we are called to bear as God's people. Besides, every day, we are called to battle against our own sins, the wicked world, and Satan and his hosts who seek to destroy us. By the end of the week, we need rest. It is for this reason that Jesus said, "The Sabbath was made for man, and not man for the Sabbath" (Mark 2:27). The Sabbath was made for man's good, physically and spiritually.

On the sabbath day, we rest when we devote ourselves to the worship of the Lord. It is for this reason that the Sabbath

is also called "the Lord's day." We set this day of the week aside for the Lord, for the worship and praise of his name. It is the Lord's day because on this day, we gather with the Lord's people for public worship. It is the Lord's day because on this day, we listen to the word of the Lord preached by our minister, a faithful servant of the Lord. It is the Lord's day because on this day, we stop doing our ordinary work and play in order to devote ourselves to the Lord.

When we properly use the earthly Sabbath, God also works in our hearts so that we long for the eternal Sabbath. That is what heaven will be—an eternal Sabbath. We will no longer need to battle against our sins. We will not face the temptations or persecution of the wicked world. Our great enemy Satan will no longer fight against us. And we will worship God perfectly, with all his people and holy angels forever. The Bible says that this is the Sabbath that remains for us as God's people (Hebrews 4:9).

Let's talk it over

1. What is the fourth commandment mainly about?

2. What does "Sabbath" mean and what is God's purpose for man in the Sabbath?

3. Is it okay for a Christian ever to miss church? When?

16. The Fifth Commandment: Honor Your Parents!

Let's read the Bible

Ephesians 6:1–9

Let's learn a Bible verse

Colossians 3:20, "Children, obey your parents in all things: for this is well pleasing unto the Lord."

Let's sing

Psalm 34, Psalter 89 in the 1912 United Presbyterian *Psalter*

Let's listen and learn

The fifth commandment is, "Honor thy father and thy mother: that thy days may be long upon the land which the LORD thy God giveth thee" (Exodus 20:12).

The fifth commandment speaks of two parents, a father and a mother—who love the Lord, who love each other for Jesus' sake, and who love their children as precious gifts from God. This is God's will for the Christian family.

The fifth commandment calls children to obey their parents. In Ephesians 6:1, the apostle Paul interpreted the fifth commandment as "children, obey your parents in the Lord." But before children obey their parents, they must honor them. That is the wording of the fifth commandment in Exodus 20:12: "*Honor* thy father and thy mother."

Honor includes obedience, but honor is more than obedience. Honor is the love and respect that you have in your heart for your parents. It isn't enough that you obey them outwardly. You must obey them out of love from your heart. Now you can see how impossible it is to obey the fifth commandment in your own strength. It is especially hard to honor and obey your parents when they are unjust or unfair. They might punish you too harshly at times. They might accuse you of doing something you did not do. But even in times like these, you must honor and obey your parents. Why? The Heidelberg Catechism gives the answer in Lord's Day 39. We "patiently bear with [our parents'] weaknesses and infirmities" because "it pleases God to govern us by their hand." You must honor and obey your parents because God set them in a place of authority over you.

Obedience to the fifth commandment continues even when you no longer live in your parents' house. When you become older, you honor and obey them by following the instruction they gave when you were younger. And when you are married and have a family of your own, you bring up your own children as your parents brought up you.

Even when your parents become very old, you obey the fifth commandment by caring for them and visiting them so that they do not become lonely.

The fifth commandment calls you to honor your parents for this reason: "that thy days may be long upon the land which the LORD thy God giveth thee."

The land God gave was the promised land of Canaan. Canaan in the Old Testament was a picture of heaven. Those who honor and obey their parents will have a place in heaven. That is an encouragement to honor your father and your mother.

Let's talk it over

1. In your own words, what is the fifth commandment?

2. What is the difference between honor and obedience?

3. When you obey your parents, whom are you really obeying? Why?

39

17. The Fifth Commandment: Honor and Obey!

Let's read the Bible

1 Peter 2:13–25

Let's learn a Bible verse

Hebrews 13:7, "Remember them which have the rule over you, who have spoken unto you the word of God: whose faith follow, considering the end of their conversation."

Let's listen and learn

The fifth commandment calls us to honor and obey our parents, or to submit to them. But God also calls us to submit to all those whom God has placed in authority over us.

In marriage, God gives authority to the husband. This is why we read in Ephesians 5:22–23, "Wives, submit yourselves to your own husbands, as unto the Lord. For the husband is the head of the wife, even as Christ is the head of the church." This does not mean that husbands may bully their wives or rule over them like tyrants. A husband must love his wife as our Lord Jesus Christ loves his church, and a husband must give his wife honor and praise for her special place in their home. In Proverbs 31:28, Solomon praised the Christian wife when he wrote, "Her children arise up, and call her blessed; her husband also, and he praiseth her."

In Bible times, some Christians were servants and even slaves. Do you know the name of the slave who ran away but whom Paul sent back to his master? That slave was Onesimus, and his master was Philemon. One day you will probably work, not as a slave for a master, but as an employee for your boss. Employees are called to submit to the authority of their bosses. You might not like everything about your job, like how many hours you have to work each day, or how much money your boss pays you for your work, but God still calls you to work faithfully and submit to your boss.

In the school that you attend, God puts teachers and the principal in the place of your parents. You are called to respect and obey your teachers just as you respect and obey your parents. That means behaving in class, studying hard, and doing your schoolwork to the best of your ability.

God also places ministers and elders over you. He calls them to rule over you and the other members of the church. And he calls all the members to submit to their rule. One way we honor and obey our minister and elders is by praying for them daily. Do you remember to pray for them?

There are also those whom God places over us in the world: the president, judges, police officers, those fighting in the armed forces, and more. Often these people are not Christians, but because God has put them in authority over you, you must submit to them, and you should pray for them. Why? The apostle Paul says that we should pray for them "that we may lead a quiet and peaceable life in all godliness and honesty" (1 Timothy 2:1–2).

There is one time when we must disobey those in authority. That one time is when those in authority require that we disobey God. Then we must say with the apostles in Acts 5:29, "We ought to obey God rather than men." Obedience to God is always first.

Let's talk it over

1. What is the calling of those who are in authority?

2. Who are our rulers in the home? In marriage? In the government? In the church?

3. What important calling does the word of God give us in 1 Timothy 2:1–2? Do you do this?

Let's sing

Psalm 82, Psalter 223 in the 1912 United Presbyterian *Psalter*

18. The Sixth Commandment: Do Not Murder!

Let's read the Bible

1 John 4:1–11

John 15:12, "This is my commandment, that ye love one another, as I have loved you."

Let's sing

Psalm 139, Psalter 383 in the 1912 United Presbyterian *Psalter*

The sixth commandment is, "Thou shalt not kill" (Exodus 20:13).

The sixth commandment forbids *murder*, the wrongful killing of another person. It often happens out of anger. An angry mob murdered Stephen because he preached about Jesus. A man might murder his neighbor because he wants something his neighbor has. King David murdered Uriah because he wanted Uriah's wife, Bathsheba, for his wife.

Sometimes parents do not want to have their baby, and they have her murdered before she is born. This is called abortion. Sometimes people do not want to care for an elderly or handicapped family member, so they have him murdered. This is called euthanasia.

Murder is far worse than taking something that is your neighbor's. It is taking your neighbor's life or your own. Murder is an attack on God, the one who gives life to each person.

Being entertained by murder is also sinful. When people watch violent television shows or play violent video games, they break the sixth commandment.

It is important to see that the sixth commandment does not only forbid murder. The commandment also forbids all the *causes* of murder—everything that leads to murder and is really murder in your heart.

Hatred is murder. If you hate someone, you think evil against them in your heart. The Bible teaches that

"whosoever hateth his brother is a murderer" (1 John 3:15). Have you ever told someone, "I hate you"? That is murder and sin against the sixth commandment.

Envy is murder. Envy is jealousy of someone who has something you do not have. Maybe you are jealous of someone because he has a better baseball glove than you or because she dresses in clothes that are more expensive than yours. In Genesis 37:11, we read that Joseph's brothers were so envious of him that they threw him into a pit and sold him as a slave into Egypt.

You can also murder someone with your words. There is a saying: "Sticks and stones can break my bones, but words can never hurt me." That's not true. Sometimes our tongues are like sharp swords that hurt and kill others by unkind words. The apostle Paul warned in Galatians 5:15, "But if ye bite and devour one another, take heed that ye be not consumed one of another."

We ought to ask ourselves whether what we are about to do, say, or think is going to help or hurt the other person. If it's going to hurt them, we are about to break the sixth commandment. We must pray to God to keep us from murdering our neighbor.

Let's talk it over

1. Why do people often murder?

2. What are some ways in which we break the sixth commandment?

3. Why is murder wrong and what makes murder such a great sin?

19. The Sixth Commandment: Love Your Neighbor!

Let's read the Bible

Luke 10:30–37

Let's learn a Bible verse

John 15:12, "This is my commandment, that ye love one another, as I have loved you."

Let's sing

Psalm 133, Psalter 371 in the 1912 United Presbyterian *Psalter*

Let's listen and learn

In the sixth commandment, God forbids murder and the causes of murder, like hatred and envy. But there is more to this commandment. In the Heidelberg Catechism, we learn that God also calls us to show patience, peace, meekness, mercy, and kindness toward *all* of our neighbors, even to our enemies (Lord's Day 40).

What is patience? If you are patient, you do not have a quick temper and you do not quickly become frustrated. The Bible tells us about two men who were very patient. When the children of Israel complained to Moses in the wilderness, he almost never grew angry with them. Job was very patient when God took everything away from him and made him very sick. He was not angry with God, but said, "The Lord gave, and the Lord hath taken away; blessed be the name of the Lord" (Job 1:21).

What is peace? Peace is the opposite of fighting. Do you live at peace with your brothers and sisters, or are you always fighting with them and making plans to get even?

What is meekness? Meekness, or humility, is the opposite of pride. If you are meek, you will not always think about how talented or how beautiful you are, but how richly God has blessed you, even though you do not deserve it.

What is kindness? Kindness is gentleness. A kind person is not always looking out for himself but is instead looking

out for others and seeking their good. Kindness shows itself in what we say and how we treat other people.

In the sixth commandment God calls you to love even your enemies. You may think that that is going a bit too far. Love your enemies—those who hate you and say bad things about you? In Luke 10:30–37, Jesus told the parable of the good Samaritan. A Jewish traveler was attacked by robbers who beat him up and left him for dead. But it was not only the robbers who were guilty of breaking the sixth commandment that day. Two others were also guilty of murder because they passed by the man and did nothing to help him. But one man had compassion on him and helped him. He was a Samaritan. This was remarkable because the Jews and the Samaritans were enemies. But that did not matter to the good Samaritan. Do you show love to your neighbor as he did?

There is one man who loved his enemies perfectly and even died in their place. Do you know who this was? It was our Lord Jesus Christ. Romans 5:10 tells us that when we were enemies, Jesus died for us, his people. As Jesus hung on the cross, he prayed for those who crucified him. Since Jesus loved those who were his enemies and prayed for them, we should do the same.

Let's talk it over

1. Moses did lose his patience once. Do you know when? How did God punish him?

2. Are you as meek and kind as you could be? What can you do to be meeker and kinder?

3. In what ways can you show love to your neighbor? How about to your enemy?

45

20. The Seventh Commandment: Do Not Commit Adultery!

Let's read the Bible

1 Corinthians 6

1 Corinthians 3:17, "If any man defile the temple of God, him shall God destroy; for the temple of God is holy, which temple ye are."

The seventh commandment is, "Thou shalt not commit adultery" (Exodus 20:14). The seventh commandment is mainly about marriage. People who are married are called to love one another in a special way. We are to love all our neighbors, but husbands and wives are to love each other with a special kind of love. The apostle Paul wrote in Ephesians 5:25, "Husbands, love your wives, even as Christ also loved the church, and gave himself for it." Paul gave this commandment to husbands, but wives must obey it, too. The husband is called to love his spouse—his wife—and the wife is called to love her spouse—her husband—just as Jesus Christ loves his church.

The special kind of love that married people have for each other is to last for life. We read in 1 Corinthians 7:39, "The wife is bound by the law as long as her husband liveth; but if her husband be dead, she is at liberty to be married to whom she will; only in the Lord." Only when someone's spouse dies may they marry again. It is wrong to divorce your wife or husband and marry someone else while your spouse is alive.

Married people commit adultery when they love someone else with the special kind of love that they are to have only for their spouse. Jesus taught that it is adultery to lust after, or desire, any person to whom you are not married. It is also sin against the seventh commandment when single people love each other with the kind of love that God reserves for those who are married. Adultery is a very serious sin.

The wicked world does not think so. It makes movies and television shows and writes books that mock marriage. They even promote adultery. But God is not pleased with people who commit adultery. In the Old Testament, this sin was punished by death.

God gave the seventh commandment to protect marriage. Marriage is a picture of Jesus' love for the church. When one man and one woman are married, they are united by God for life. In marriage, husband and wife must encourage and help each other bear all the troubles, sorrows, and difficulties that come upon them in this life. Often God blesses the marriages of his people with children. Husbands and wives must be faithful to each other also for their children's sake. When husbands and wives divorce, there are always sad consequences for their children.

Although the seventh commandment mainly has to do with married people, it does not only have to do with them. It also has something to say to single people. Single people, too, must never forget that their bodies are temples of the Lord. We must respect our bodies as gifts from God and use them for God's glory.

Let's talk it over

1. What is marriage? What is adultery?

2. Why do you think that the devil and the world attack marriage?

3. What does this commandment teach those who are not married?

Let's sing

Psalm 45, Psalter 125 in the 1912 United Presbyterian *Psalter*

21. The Seventh Commandment: Husbands, Love Your Wives!

Let's read the Bible

Ephesians 5:21–33

Let's listen and learn

The seventh commandment forbids adultery. By forbidding adultery, the seventh commandment protects marriage. The seventh commandment, and the rest of holy Scripture, teach us about God's will for marriage. What is God's will for marriage? How does God call Christian husbands and wives to live?

The first very important truth about marriage is that God calls his people to marry in the Lord (1 Corinthians 7:39). That means that Christian young men are only to marry Christian young women. And that means that Christian young women are only to marry Christian young men. This is also the apostle Paul's teaching in Ephesians 5. There he

teaches us that our marriages are to be a picture of Jesus and his bride, the church. But how can that be, if the husband or wife is not a child of God?

Often God's people in the Old Testament got into serious trouble because they married ungodly people. In the days of Noah, the wickedness of man was so great that God destroyed the world with the flood. One cause of that great wickedness was that the young men and women of the church did not marry in the Lord. We read in Genesis 6:2, "That the sons of God saw the daughters of men that they were fair; and they took them wives of all which they chose."

But it is not enough that Christians marry in the Lord. Christian husbands must love their wives and always deal with them in love, just as our Lord Jesus Christ loves his church. Husbands must show love to their wives by how they treat them. The apostle Paul wrote in Ephesians 5:29 that husbands must "nourish" and "cherish" their wives. That means they must be kind to them, encouraging, and gentle, just as Jesus is kind, encouraging, and gentle toward his church.

Christian wives must also love their husbands. Usually when a husband loves his wife, she will also love him. Isn't that the way it is with Jesus and his church? Whose love is first? Whose love is a response to the other's love? If everything is right in a marriage and a husband loves his wife, she will also love him. Then in the love that she has for her husband, a wife must minister to her husband's needs and to the needs of her family. She must be a faithful helper to her husband. And she must submit to her husband, just as we submit to Jesus Christ. When husbands and wives love each other and live with each other as they ought, they give a beautiful picture of Jesus Christ and his bride, the church.

Let's learn a Bible verse

Ephesians 5:33, "Nevertheless let everyone of you in particular so love his wife even as himself; and the wife see that she reverence her husband."

Let's talk it over

1. What does it mean to marry in the Lord?

2. What is the calling of a Christian husband?

3. What is the calling of a Christian wife?

Let's sing

Psalm 128, Psalter 360 in the 1912 United Presbyterian *Psalter*

49

22. The Eighth Commandment: Do Not Steal!

Let's read the Bible

Malachi 3:6–12

Matthew 21:13, "And said unto them, It is written, My house shall be called the house of prayer; but ye have made it a den of thieves."

The eighth commandment is, "Thou shalt not steal" (Exodus 20:15). Stealing is taking for ourselves what God has given to someone else. Someone who steals is called a robber or a thief.

There are different ways to steal. It isn't only bank robbers who break the eighth commandment. The commandment forbids stealing anything that belongs to someone else, whether it belongs to your brother or sister, your classmate, your neighbor, your boss, or the grocery store. Taking someone's bicycle, baseball, or backpack is forbidden. It is also wrong to use ideas from a book or off the internet in school without saying where they came from. Copying someone else's homework or their answers on a test is also stealing. If you take someone else's ideas or answers but let your teacher think that they are your answers and ideas, you are cheating. Cheating is lying, but it is also stealing.

Another way we steal is by wasting our time. Everything we have is given to us by God. Our time is no different. We must use our time wisely. If we do not use the time our teacher gives us to work on an assignment, we are guilty of stealing. A father who is lazy and does not spend his time working hard to provide for his family is guilty of stealing. A mother who wastes her time when she should be taking care of her children and her home is also guilty of stealing. Teenagers who spend many hours on their phones rather than doing their homework or helping around the house are stealing. The Bible does not say that you may never play, or spend time relaxing, or go on vacation. But it does say that you may not do these things when you should be working.

It is also possible to steal from God. This happens when Christians do not give their offerings to the church. Israel in the Old Testament was guilty of this kind of stealing. The prophet Malachi said, "Will a man rob God? Yet ye have robbed me. But ye say, Wherein have we robbed thee? In tithes and offerings. Ye are cursed with a curse: for ye have robbed me, even this whole nation" (Malachi 3:8–9).

The eighth commandment is a serious warning to every Christian. We must not steal! And we must repent of the many times when we have stolen from God and from our neighbor. At the same time, we must never forget that Jesus died for thieves. In fact, he was crucified between two thieves. One of those thieves repented and was saved. For this sin there is forgiveness in our Lord Jesus Christ.

Let's talk it over

1. What is the sin of stealing?

2. Why is it wrong to steal? What if the person from whom you steal is rich and won't miss it anyway?

3. How do people steal from God?

Let's sing

Psalm 15, Psalter 24 in the 1912 United Presbyterian *Psalter*

23. The Eighth Commandment: Be a Faithful Steward!

Let's read the Bible

Ephesians 4:20–32

Let's learn a Bible verse

Psalm 24:1, "The earth is the LORD's, and the fulness thereof; the world, and they that dwell therein."

Let's listen and learn

The eighth commandment forbids stealing. We may not take what belongs to someone else. We may not be thieves and robbers. Instead we are called to be God's stewards. In Bible times, a steward was a very special servant. Usually a steward worked for a king or a rich nobleman. The steward had charge of all the property and possessions of his master. He was also head over all the other servants. At all times, he was to seek the good of his master.

The Bible gives us several examples of stewards. Eliezer was Abraham's steward. Abraham even trusted Eliezer to find a god-fearing wife for his son, Isaac. Joseph became the steward of an important Egyptian named Potiphar. Genesis 39:4 tells us that Potiphar, "made [Joseph] overseer over his house, and all that he had he put into his hand."

As God's stewards, we must understand that all that we own is given to us by God. God gives every Christian some of the things of this world, but none of these things are really ours. God gives to one Christian more, so that he is rich. God gives less to another, so that he is poor. In 1 Samuel 2:7, we read: "The LORD maketh poor, and maketh rich: he bringeth low, and lifteth up." The important thing to understand is that whether we are rich or poor, all that we have is given to us by God.

Because God gives us whatever we have, we must be content. That means we are happy and satisfied with what he has given us. The person who is content is not jealous of others and is not going to steal.

Contentment does not mean that we may not work hard so that we can enjoy a better earthly life and more possessions than we have right now. A faithful husband and father will work hard for the good of his family. But in the meantime, he and his family will always be satisfied with what God has given them. You may work hard too, to earn enough money to buy a new bicycle, baseball glove, necklace, or dress someday. But in the meantime, you must be content with the things that God has given you.

Because we are stewards, we must use the things God gives us for his glory. Our cars and clothes, furniture and food, jeans and jewelry—it all belongs to God. We must use everything to serve him. Solomon wrote that we must "honor the LORD with [our] substance [and]...increase: so shall thy barns be filled with plenty, and thy presses shall burst out with new wine" (Proverbs 3:9–10). This does not mean that everyone who is a good steward always has great riches. Job feared God, but God took everything away from Job. The meaning is that God will bless us when we live as good stewards. This blessing is especially knowing that God is pleased with us.

Let's talk it over

1. What does it mean that we are God's stewards?

2. Who really owns everything that we consider to be ours?

3. Since we are God's stewards, we are to use all things to his glory. Give an example of this from your own life.

Let's sing

Psalm 37, Psalter 101 in the 1912 United Presbyterian *Psalter*

53

24. The Ninth Commandment: Do Not Lie!

Let's read the Bible

Proverbs 12:13–28

Let's learn a Bible verse

Psalm 141:3, "Set a watch, O LORD, before my mouth; keep the door of my lips."

Let's listen and learn

The ninth commandment is, "Thou shalt not bear false witness against thy neighbor" (Exodus 20:16). The ninth commandment forbids lying. Bearing false witness is lying.

What is a lie? A lie is something that is not true, an untruth. But not every untruth is a lie. You might mistakenly write on a math paper that 4 + 3 = 8. That is an untruth, and your teacher will mark your answer wrong. But it is not a lie. A lie is a *deliberate* untruth. You know what the truth is. But you deliberately change the truth.

Often people lie to cover up a sin or avoid punishment. How often haven't you done that? You were being mean to your sister or brother, but when your mother asks you about it, you lie. You deny that you said or did anything mean. Or maybe a classmate tells the teacher that you said a bad word on the playground. When the teacher talks to you about this, you deny it because you don't want to get into trouble. That is the sin of lying.

Earlier you learned that the sin of cheating is stealing. But cheating is also lying. When you cheat, you make your teacher believe that this is your answer, or the assignment that you completed, or the test answers that you wrote.

And then there is the sin of gossip, the sin of spreading rumors about people. This sin shows itself in two ways. You may be speaking the truth about someone to others, but even though it's the truth, it is hurtful. This sin is called backbiting. Or the rumor may be false. The person did not say what you report they said or do what you said they did. Gossip that is a lie is called slander.

And then there is the person who lives a lie. They pretend that they are someone whom they are not. This happens in the church. Someone pretends to be a Christian, pretends to love God, and pretends to love the church. But it is a lie. He is a hypocrite. This was true of Ananias and Sapphira in the early history of the New Testament church. They lied to the apostles when they gave to the church only part of the money from selling a piece of land. Their sin was not that they kept back part of the money, but that they told the apostles they were giving them *all* the money from selling the land.

Every day the child of God ought to pray the prayer of the psalmist in Psalm 141:3, "Set a watch, O LORD, before my mouth; keep the door of my lips."

Let's talk it over

1. What is the sin condemned in the ninth commandment? What is lying?

2. What is backbiting? What is slander?

3. What should you do if you tell a lie? What should you do if you find out that someone has told you a lie?

Let's sing

Psalm 101, Psalter 271 in the 1912 United Presbyterian *Psalter*

25. The Ninth Commandment: Speak the Truth in Love!

Let's read the Bible

James 3:1–10

Let's learn a Bible verse

Ephesians 4:15, "But speaking the truth in love, may grow up into him in all things, which is the head, even Christ."

Let's listen and learn

In Ephesians 4:15, Paul called Christians to keep the ninth commandment when he instructed them to "speak the truth in love." Our tongues have been created by God. What a wonderful thing that God has made us to speak. That makes us different than the animals—very different. We can use words to teach, to ask questions, to give commands, and to offer encouragement. There are so many uses of our tongues and of our words. But what we must never forget is that *God* gave us our tongues. We must use them to speak the truth for God's glory and for the good of others.

We must speak the truth that God is the only true God, that God's word is truth, that God's Son Jesus is the only Savior. We must also speak the truth about ourselves—never lying to impress people with how great we are. And we must speak the truth about others so that we never put them down or make them look bad. Solomon wrote in Proverbs 12:22, "Lying lips are an abomination to the Lord: but they that deal truly are his delight."

We must speak the truth to one another *in love*. God calls us to love him and our neighbor. That is the great commandment behind each of the Ten Commandments. When we speak, we must ask ourselves, "Does what I am about to say come out of a heart that loves my neighbor?" If you cannot say yes to that question, you should not speak.

Love for the neighbor always shows itself in what we say and how we talk. If a husband loves his wife, he shows it in how he talks to her. He is kind in his words. When she is discouraged, he will speak words of encouragement to her. Parents who love their children speak to them in such a way that they hear love in their parents' voices. Brothers and sisters who love one another do not mock, tease, or insult one another. And members of the church who love one another use their words to build each other up, not tear each other down.

The will of God in the ninth commandment makes us long for heaven. In Revelation 5:13, the apostle John had a vision of every creature in heaven and on earth saying, "Blessing, and honor, and glory, and power, be unto him that sitteth upon the throne, and unto the Lamb for ever and ever." In heaven, our tongues will finally speak the truth in love perfectly because we will speak only the praises of God.

Let's talk it over

1. How are we called to use our tongues?

2. How are we called to speak to one another?

3. Who hears every word that we say? Do you very often think of this?

Let's sing

Psalm 141, Psalter 386 in the 1912 United Presbyterian *Psalter*

26. The Tenth Commandment: Do Not Covet!

Let's read the Bible

Joshua 7

Let's learn a Bible verse

Psalm 119:36, "Incline my heart unto thy testimonies, and not to covetousness."

Let's listen and learn

The tenth commandment is found in Deuteronomy 5:21. The commandment begins, "Thou shalt not desire." Desiring something in your heart is also called coveting.

The tenth commandment is also found in Exodus 20:17, where we read, "Thou shalt not covet thy neighbor's house, thou shalt not covet thy neighbor's wife, nor his manservant, nor his maidservant, nor his ox, nor his ass, nor anything that is thy neighbor's." Sometimes people wonder why the tenth commandment mentions our neighbor's *house* first, not his wife. Isn't his wife more important than his house? Shouldn't she be mentioned first? The word "house" in the tenth commandment is not the building in which we live. "House" is really "household" or "family." And then the most important person in the household is mentioned first, the wife.

The first nine commandments concern our outward deeds—what we say and what we do. These commandments certainly include our heart, thoughts, and desires. But these commandments themselves speak of our actions. Bowing down to an idol, taking God's name in vain, disobeying parents, committing adultery, stealing, and lying are all outward deeds. The tenth commandment is different than the other nine. It concerns the heart. The tenth commandment forbids evil desires in your heart and calls you instead to desire to please God.

Coveting or desiring is not wrong itself. Because of the way God has made us, we cannot help desiring. We desire all the time. When you woke up this morning, you desired to get up and get dressed. You desired to eat your breakfast and go to school if it was a school day. You desired to see your friends and your teacher. The Bible even calls us to covet. The apostle Paul taught the church at Corinth to "covet earnestly the best gifts" (1 Corinthians 12:31). We are to desire the best spiritual gifts of God. And in 1 Peter 2:2, the apostle Peter called Christians to be like "newborn babes [and] desire the sincere milk of the word, that ye may grow thereby." The word "desire" here is really "covet." As children of God, we are to covet the pure milk of God's word in order to grow as healthy, strong Christians.

It is not wrong to covet. But what are you coveting? That is the question. What do you desire? What have you set your heart on? The tenth commandment forbids *sinful* coveting. It forbids coveting the things which belong to your neighbor.

Let's talk it over

1. What does it mean to covet?

2. Is coveting always wrong? Explain your answer.

3. Are there things that we ought to covet? Can you think of any examples?

Let's sing

Psalm 86, Psalter 236 in the 1912 United Presbyterian *Psalter*

27. The Tenth Commandment: Love God with Your Whole Heart!

Let's read the Bible

Luke 12:13–21

Hebrews 13:5, "Let your conversation be without covetousness; and be content with such things as ye have: for he hath said, I will never leave thee, nor forsake thee."

The tenth commandment forbids sinful coveting—desiring the things that belong to our neighbor. When the Bible refers to sinful coveting, it often calls it "lust." Numbers 11 tells the story of the children of Israel lusting for food in the wilderness. God sent them quails for food, but he also sent a very great plague that killed many of them. At the end of Numbers 11, we read that "there they buried the people that lusted" (v. 34).

Sinful coveting includes several things. First, we may not desire that which God has given to our neighbor. For children, it might be his bicycle or baseball glove, her dress or her bracelet. For young people, it might be clothes or a car. For grownups, it might be money, a house, or a camping trailer. And coveting isn't only desiring the *things* that belong to someone else. We might be jealous of their popularity, their athletic ability, how smart they are, or their good looks.

It is also coveting to seek after earthly things themselves. "Thou shalt not covet" means that we are not to be consumed with having earthly things, nor with doing everything we can to get what we want. The Bible warns in 1 John 2:15, "Love not the world, neither the things that are in the world. If any man love the world, the love of the Father is not in him."

Although sinful coveting is a matter of the heart— something that we can hide and keep secret in our heart— sooner or later it becomes plain that someone is gripped by

covetousness. His thoughts are all about this world and the things of this world. When he is in school, or riding on the bus, or driving down the road, or sitting in church, this is what is always on his mind.

Covetousness also shows itself when a person is unwilling to part with the things of this world. Maybe that person loses his possessions in some terrible disaster like a fire. Maybe a thief steals his possessions from him. The result is that the person becomes very upset, angry, and even bitter.

A sure sign that a person is covetous is that his or her desire to be rich and to gather earthly possessions gets in the way of the worship of God. He has no time for reading the Bible, attending Bible studies, or praying. She is exhausted from working so many hours during the week, that she oversleeps on Sunday morning rather than going to church. When a person's worship of God suffers, that is a sure sign that he is consumed with covetousness. Nothing should get in the way of our faithful worship of God.

Let's talk it over

1. Give some examples of sinful coveting.

2. Although sinful coveting is a matter of the heart, how does sinful coveting show itself?

3. Are there any indications in your life that you are guilty of sinful coveting?

Let's sing

Psalm 119, Psalter 321 in the 1912 United Presbyterian *Psalter*

28. The Tenth Commandment: God Sees and God Knows!

Let's read the Bible

1 Corinthians 2:1–9

1 Corinthians 2:9, "But as it is written, Eye hath not seen, nor ear heard, neither have entered into the heart of man, the things which God hath prepared for them that love him."

The tenth and last commandment of God's law condemns sinful coveting. Sinful coveting is desiring in our hearts what belongs to someone else and what God has not been pleased to give to us. From the tenth commandment, we learn a number of important things.

One thing we learn is that God sees and knows our *hearts*. God does not only see and know what we *do*. He sees more— much more. He sees and knows what is in our hearts. God does not only want us to keep his law outwardly. Oh, no! He wants us to keep his law from our hearts.

We also learn from the tenth commandment that God is not only concerned with what we do. He is concerned with our motives, or why we do what we do. He does not only look at the deed. He also looks at the reason for doing the deed. Only when the motive is pure is the deed good in the sight of God. It is not enough that we obey our parents. We must obey them for the right reason. It is not enough that we are in church on Sunday. God sees into our hearts and knows whether we have come to church for the right reason. God does not only hear what we say about someone. He sees into our hearts and knows the motive behind what we have said.

The tenth commandment also teaches us that the law of God calls us to a life of love for God and for others. This love is not only right words we say about God and kind words we say about others. This love is not only good deeds we do in the name of God and for others. But we are called to love God and others from our hearts. This is what God sees in us and knows about us. He sees and knows whether we love him and whether we love our neighbor.

We are to love God and others before ourselves. The great sin that the tenth commandment warns against is not love of the things of the world. But it is love for ourselves—love for ourselves more than we love God or love for ourselves more than we love anyone else. We must learn to deny ourselves and seek the good of others before ourselves.

When we do set our heart upon the things of this earth and we do love ourselves more than God, there is only one remedy. The remedy is that we understand our one great need: our need for God and his word. This is why we must desire God more than anything else. In him and in his Son, our Lord Jesus Christ, all our needs are met. On the cross, Jesus Christ obtained for us riches beyond anything that can be found in this world—the eternal riches of salvation.

Let's talk it over

1. What does God teach us in the tenth commandment that he sees and knows?

2. Do you think about this very often, that God sees and knows your heart?

3. What does it mean that God knows our motives?

Let's sing

Psalm 147, Psalter 403 in the 1912 United Presbyterian *Psalter*